Kinds of Affection

Kinds

of

Affection

By JOSEPHINE MILES

Wesleyan University Press

MIDDLETOWN, CONNECTICUT

Many of these poems have appeared elsewhere. For permission to reprint, and for assigning copyrights, grateful acknowledgment is made to the editors and publishers of *The Atlantic Monthly, Carleton Miscellany, The Nation, Northwest Review, Quarterly Review of Literature,* and *Uclan Review;* also to Basic Books, Inc., publisher of *Of Poetry and Power* edited by Erwin A. Glikes and Paul Schwaber; and to *Oyez,* Berkeley, California.

The following poems, under the titles given in parentheses, first appeared in *Poetry:* "After I come home from a meeting with friends" ("Turn"), "Apart from branches in courtyards and small stones" ("Countryside"), "Does the world look like a park to you?" ("Park"), "Down from another planet they have settled to mend" ("Album"), "I walked along the river path, the river" ("King"), "Looking over toward Tamalpais" ("Sunday"), "Love at a distance can mean," "Still early morning, the wind's edge" ("Edge"), "Who called brought to my mind the name of power" ("Power"), and "A woman with a basket was walking" ("Rehearsal").

The following, similarly identified, were first printed in *The Massachusetts Review:* "Addicts progress from saturation" ("Greed"), "In a morning of clarity and distinction" ("Clear Day"), and "So you are thinking of principles to go on" ("A Conversation with Alexander Meiklejohn").

The five poems under the general title "In dialogues of modus vivendi" were initially published in *Chelsea.*

The three poems under the general title "From Hindi"—"A Star Quivered" by Kirti Chan-huri, "You Are Alone" by Ajit Kumar, and "The Family" by Vishwanath—are copyright © 1965 by Indiana University Press; reprinted by permission of the publisher from *Modern Hindi Poetry* edited by Vidya Niwas Misra.

Library of Congress Catalog Card Number : 67–24108

Manufactured in the United States of America

First edition

Contents (First lines)

When I telephoned a friend, her husband told me   11

A woman with a basket was walking   16

He wakes up in his town, he looks at it   17

The mailman is coming from the next block down   20

Bodily kindness is common; though some   21

Love at a distance can mean   22

After I come home from a meeting with friends   23

In a morning of clarity and distinction   24

Friends in our questions, we looked together   25

Who called brought to my mind the name of power   26

Addicts progress from saturation   27

Grievances: the warm fogs of summer   28

I've been going around everywhere without any skin   29

Someone, an engineer, told a confab of wires   30

Who shall we raise up, who glorify—our wounded   31

The doctor who sits at the bedside of a rat   32

The entrepreneur chicken shed his tail feathers, surplus   33

In dialogues of modus vivendi:

       I. Four old men standing around in the yard   34

       II. Blast, says the neighbor at the gate   35

       III. The studies you tend to favor   36

       IV. CASTOR: Planetary! That is my vision   38

       V. You must go no further on this dangerous way   39

We have the generation which carries something new not far enough   41

The life of Galileo as it is reset   42

What do you think caused the disaster here   43

I fear to take a step; along the edge   44

After noon I lie down   45

Marin mousebait contains warfarin   46

Daniel Boone stepped up to a window   47

As difference blends into identity   49

In the town where every man is king   50

I walked along the river path, the river   51

Throwing his life away   52

So you are thinking of principles to go on   53

From Hindi:

     I. A star quivered in a corner of the sky   57

     II. . . . But the accursed twilight came   57

     III. My father   58

Looking over toward Tamalpais   59

Along the street where we used to stop for bread   60

Dear Frank, Here is a poem   61

Still early morning, the wind's edge   62

When Sanders brings feed to his chickens, some sparrows   63

Apart from branches in courtyards and small stones   64

When the sun came up, the rooster expanded to meet it   65

How goes a crowd where it goes?   66

The leaf is growing   67

Does the world look like a park to you? Yes, almost suddenly   68

Every day when she came to the steps that led   69

I am trying to think what it means to be right 70

Bucking and rolling, the ship bent 72

In the neighborhood of my childhood, a hundred lungers 73

Down from another planet they have settled to mend 74

Yesterday evening as the sun set late 75

When I was eight, I put in the left-hand drawer 76

Truth is never 77

Have I outgrown you? 78

Kinds of Affection

When I telephoned a friend, her husband told me
     She's not here tonight, she's out saving the Bay.
     She is sitting and listening in committee chambers,
     Maybe speaking, with her light voice
     From the fourteenth row, about where
     The birds and fish will go if we fill in the Bay.

     The fish, she says, include starry flounder,
     Pacific herring, rockfish, surfperches,
     And the flat fish who come to the spawning flats
     In the shallow waters near the narrow shores.
     The shadow-look you know, the fish shooting
     In that light green shallow, a dark arrow.

     Otherwise we will get a bowling alley,
     A car park and golf course, with financing,
     Sift up the shallows into a solid base
     With sand dredged from the deeper channels, brought in scows
     Or hopper dredges, and dumped on the fish, and then paved over
     For recreation with no cost to the city.

     And so we hear the sides, the margins speaking:
     To allow the Commission in the public interest
     Permits for the recovery of sand and gravel
     From the submerged tidelands of the state,
     Fill of unlimited quality, clean sand
     Replenished by the southern littoral drift;

     Or yet, Dear Sirs: Your bill flies in the face
     Of the U.S. Army Engineers' Barrier Study,
     The Delta Study, Transportation Study,
     Even the Petroleum Institute plan for bringing freighters
     And hundreds of workers in to Contra Costa
     To boat, bathe, drink, and return these waters.

11

A student I remember said to me, My mother
Wants me to be a banker, but I want to be
A sanitary engineer, spending all that money
Back toward the sea. Do you think it's possible?
See how these hills shape down back of the college
In summer streaked with little dry arroyos,
In winter running over, rush and freshet,
Through storm drains, cellars, sometimes parlors, straight
    away
Down to the sea. Think of the veins
Of this earth all flowing raining water,
The drove of rivers in the pipes we've laid.

Effluent, said my student, there's a word.
Give me a choice between it and *débris*
And any day I'd choose *effluent.*
Cover and fill is bleach and burn, with tires
Sticking up out of the muck, and loads
Of old brush and tree branches crisping away there.
Not for me, I like the purest water
Sparkling green under a soil, and it can breeze
Out of our pipes and chemicals, lucent as
The rain itself, around the bodies
Of fish and swimmers.

Saving the bay,
Saving the shoals of day,
Saving the tides of shallows deep begun
Between the moon and sun.

Saving the sidings of the Santa Fé.
Saving the egret and the herring run,

Cane and acacia, mallow and yarrow save,
Against the seventh wave,

Boundary and margin, meeting and met,
So that the pure sea will not forget,
Voracious as it is, its foreign kind,
And so the land,

Voracious as it is, will not redeem
Another's diadem.
Saving the shores,
Saving the lines between

Kelp, shrimp, and the scrub green,
Between the lap of waters
And the long
Shoulder of stone.

Therein, between, no homogeneous dredge,
But seedy edge
Of action and of chance
Met to its multiple and variable circumstance.

Though a news column says that Aquatic Park is a police
    headache,
In the past year, eighty-seven arrests
Of characters for crimes better not talked about,
That the lake is a favorite dumping spot for hot safes,
Burglary tools, stripped bikes, even a body,

Yet a notice says, Next week at Aquatic Park,
The V-Drive Boating Club holds its annual race—
Everybody comes out for this event—

These are the world's fastest boats, faster than hydros,
Needing the quiet water the embankment provides.

And a letter from a statistician, fond of the facts,
Compares the use of Aquatic Park to the Rose Garden:
        the same pattern;
Fewest people, about five each, on a Friday of terrible
        weather,
Next, about fifty, on a warm Wednesday afternoon,
Most, a hundred and fifty, on a clear windy Saturday.
        Signed, sincerely, Statistician.

Some live in the deeps, a freighter
Plying between here and Yokohama.
Some live in the rose gardens,
Deeps of a street, a two-storied
Observer and participant, daily
Moving out into the traffic, back into it
Where curtains billow in their breakfast room.
The deeps. Some
Live in the margins. Have they the golden mean?

Freight whistles reach here and the fire engines
Coming from town, foundry hammers
Among the wash of waves.
Kelp drifts them up afloat, and suddenly
They are in the tinder world of lizards.
Cut ashore they bask and breathe
And then plunge back
Down the long glints that take their weight.
At home. At home. But which?

Likely a sea captain will live in a margin
But never wants to, wants a deep molded farm;

Likely an architect, but mainly weekends.
On the weekdays, along the Bay margin
Little happens, small objects
Breed and forage. Flights come in and vanish.
Solicitudes entail solicitudes.
Dredge the channel, reinforce the sea wall
And we shall have deep calling to deep directly.

She starts to speak, my friend in her light voice,
Of margins: marshes, birds, and embarcaderos.
Truths spread to dry like nets, mended like nets,
Draw in at the edges their corruptions,
To let the moving world of bay and town
Mingle, as they were amphibian again.

Saving the bay. Saving the blasted bay.
That there be margins of the difference,
Scrap heap and mobile, wind ridge and ledge,
Mud and débris. That there be
Shore and sea.

A woman with a basket was walking
  In the aisle of the rehearsal.
  What did she carry to whom in that aisle?
  Also three girls I had never seen before, though I came often
  Because I had written the play.

  At random scattered through the lighted
  Well where the dark should be, many others
  Of indefinable and nonchalant purpose.
  I stared at them, but they
  Did not look at the play.

  One was crocheting; I've not seen crocheting
  For many years. One brought a message,
  A whispered conference followed, and a few went out.
  There was a man reading music there
  And a boy with a dog.

  The intense miscellaneities and haphazard sidelines
  Of the rehearsal troubled me, how they diffused
  The cast's dedication to its lines.
  Now look—the first-night curtain rising
  Discloses as performers in this play

  Boy, dog, man, music, woman with basket
  Conveying what to whom on what aisle?

He wakes up in his town, he looks at it,
    Hotel Victoria, Bamboo Café, river
    Broad as a dream, between willows.
    Anyone
    Could float down it wreathed in flowers.
    He goes to the merchants' luncheons, he is a merchant,
    And says, as the long dust stifles roads and meetings,
    And the springtime day wears on in a tedium of dry parity,
    Remember, we are on the Avon,
    The Canadian Avon;
    A poor girl could float down it with flowers,
    Rosemary for remembrance.
    He doesn't know much about the theater,
    But he knows what he likes.

    Eventually he goes straight to the watershed
    Of Stratford, England, by train and plane,
    And brings from his source designers and performers,
    So that after the bitter cold lets up,
    The plains and streets no longer clogged with snow,
    The trilliums again in their coverts,
    Tights, doublets, motley come forward from the proscenium
        by the river
    And address the members of the Chamber of Commerce.
    A Shakespearean teashop sets up on Center Street,
    Motels add units.
    In rummage and parade, women and children
    Move toward fund raising.
    Othello Braves, Elsinore Indians,
    Participate in their own renascence.

    Ophelia
    Hears the quiet and the drowsy river
    A block from town

Murmuring its blank pentameter.
Soft drinks upon the drought of road and field
Bless and are blessed. Yellow buses
Bear in across the plains from larger centers
Hundreds of Torontons in the twilight
In silks, dress kilts, Bermuda shorts.
No place to sleep, they drive through the long midnight,
No place to eat, they picnic in the park,
They are an audience like a sudden, regular
Twice-daily horde; they consume
With a voracity of crickets.

Sometimes as Touchstone is fishing
In the river of the Forest of Arden, the Avon,
A little boy
Alone among the voracious thousands, laughs.
That is his contribution of dollars. The old clowns
Give him back its weight in more fishing.
Such a lot of fishing would upset a show
Were it not Arden.
As it is Arden, a great splash
Splashes in the aisles in the warmth of summer.
Sometimes too the Kings of England flourish,
History recurs; Lancaster reviews his forces,
Richard and Henry in the Chamber of Commerce
Exalt the imagination of their hosts.

To his ears
Deaf from the winds and roads across Ontario,
Dull with the dusty sounds of dusty voices,
Runs the slow shallow river of the Avon
Carrying yet Ophelia
Speaking her springtime lines into the luncheon,
Till he becomes

In some renewed degree of transformation
Up to Toronto for funds, over to London,
Back from Moscow with dancers, out of the Bamboo Café
For pop in the park —
Orlando,
Comedy's hero in his tent of summer,
Summer's architect in his wide pavilion.

The mailman is coming from the next block down,
    Where the sycamores thin out and flowering plums
    Begin. A little boy's mother is terrified as he beats his head
    On the pavement in anger. She is crying, Softer.

    From the next block down, where flowering plums
    Thin to industrial fog, coconut soap on the cottages,
    A great morning squabble races
    In which the big machines call, Softer.

    One letter from the merchants' association asks:
    How improve status in its concrete forms
    Without demolition? How does the Vogue Cleaners
    Sponge off the spot without fraying the coat?

    One from the emporium of knowledge:
    How can we not corrupt answers with questions
    And clearly enough say to the coasting pavement,
    Keep off the grass?

    One from the hill: What do we do
    When the formulas buckle
    And men beat their heads on the pavement
    In pure anger? write them a letter?

    One third-class ad from the snowfields of the Sierras,
    The mailman's birthplace, he says, comes cool
    Across orchards to the bay to say to his readers, Softer,
    Softer.

Bodily kindness is common; though some
    Kindness has no bodily motion, in some
    Hand's touch of hand, foot's of ground,
    Rib's of air,
    The self flowers easily.

    Some unkindness as of wrath can be worldly,
    Brusque interiors of alienation, solid
    Resistance, and a twisting hate
    Of stem for stem. But close to
    Paradise is the moving body of self.

Love at a distance can mean
    Love of a dozen
    Students sitting around for the last time
    Before summer, to come no more,
    Tired and sore,
    Yet to be loved in their measureless aptitude.

    Love at a distance can be the good
    Work done by a workman, so simplified
    He could not do better if he tried;
    So austere, thank or praise
    Only by use.
    Or can be the distance at which you measureless move.

    That is, far off.
    So that love can be drawn
    In filaments of thought, in lines as thin
    As the lines latitudes rest upon.
    From plenty, from perfection, marking these
    Measureless distances.

After I come home from the meeting with friends
    I lie to sleep on the turn of the earth as it spins
    Toward the sun, toward the rising light as the day begins
    And think of those I love as the day ends.

    They are clearing the dishes, sweeping the ashes away,
    They are threading the traffic, moving toward distances,
    Disposing their hearts as the dark midnight spins,
    Gathering toward the light of the new day.

    Spent and regained, their strength for a cause, for a plain
    Defeat or delight, strengthens my heart as it moves
    Into sleep, and my sleep as it runs in the grooves
    Toward the east where a waking heart is more than mine.

In a morning of clarity and distinction
    Students and I exchange questions and answers about a book
    As if we had all been reading it.

    Then stepping over a rough place
    I hold out my hand for balance, and someone gives it.
    And someone writes a letter for help I can give.

    Late in the day, spare of shadow,
    A camera comes to report a face
    I cannot assent to; the camera

    Assents. May I
    Tomorrow, shady or turbulent,
    Keep this day's simple fact it grants to me.

Friends in our questions, we looked together
    At several mysteries,
    And argued at them long and lightly, whether
    Their no or yes.

    Now one of us is sure, another's question
    Turns counterfeit,
    Unnegotiable in a redemption
    By if or yet.

    Wish that the future in its mysterious motion
    Will come and will
    Bring sureness to us all in our devotion,
    But though, but still.

Who called brought to my mind the name of power,
    Who loves its name.
    Power.
    It must not reck or rue
    But does unto
    As cannot unto it be done the same.

    All one way move the traffic lanes of power.
    It receives
    Leadings, and drives them on,
    Gifts and rapidly gives
    Them on,
    Knowing how it is giving which receives.

    Happily, power in its operation
    Often is given
    More than it allows.
    Out of its many empires, one empire,
    Whether or not power knows,
    Puts in its hand its one life's simple portion.

Addicts progress from saturation
    To saturation, ache, thirst, slake,
    To a plenitude, an oblivion, then they wake
    And ache, until gradually as the sun climbs the heavens
    They thirst again toward that oblivion.

    Greed of the addict will intensify
    And enlarge its wants beyond certainty; I
    Am not so greedy; when I can be
    A moment glad, repletion
    Lasts me the day through, or so I say.

    Nibbling greed, must I not resent
    Your petty privileges, meagre consent,
    That certify your set of sequences?
    Seek me to free you and myself from this
    Addiction to a pure hypothesis.

Grievances: the warm fogs of summer
    Preserve them on the bough; finally a chill
    Reason sends them flying off and away.

    I keep one or two and press them in a book,
    And when I show them to you they have crumbled
    To powder on the page. So I rehearse.

    But I do not believe. I believe rather,
    The stems of grievance put down their heavy roots
    And by the end of summer crack the pavement.

I've been going around everywhere without any skin
    And it hurts. The winds hurts. Any touch.
    Attitudes distant from my own look out and find me.
    When I see a face a long way off, my forehead blisters.
    Raw the hot flesh under skin.

    Now I am going to live so deep down in
    That my skin will be a lost harm like Algeria.
    Down in will be craters, violences to be tolerated
    By other violences. Not by you,
    Not by country or climate, this personal flaying.

Someone, an engineer, told a confab of wires
    How blood flows; wove and tied the wires
    To small motors. Then the pads and motors
    Rode the beltline to the wholesale world.

    I came in tired, crossed with enigmas,
    Hextuplicate petitions, forgetting how blood flows.
    Then said the engineer to his rememberer,
    Go ahead, remind her, for auld lang syne.

Who shall we raise up, who glorify—our wounded,
    After we have deepened and explored the wound.
    He will be object of our ministration
    Who needs it most as we define his need.

    Tenderness, how it comes in a rush to aid us,
    Like an appetite, to satiety,
    After we instance to our satisfaction
    The sufferer more recipient than we.

    We have disarmed him, now we can help him,
    Have shown him wrong, now he may seek redress.
    Ready hearts, we offer to his service
    The power of professional righteousness.

The doctor who sits at the bedside of a rat
    Obtains real answers—a paw twitch,
    An ear tremor, a gain or loss of weight,
    No problem as to which
    Is temper and which is true.
    What a rat feels, he will do.

    Concomitantly then, the doctor who sits
    At the bedside of a rat
    Asks real questions, as befits
    The place, like where did that potassium go, not what
    Do you think of Willie Mays or the weather?
    So rat and doctor may converse together.

The entrepreneur chicken shed his tail feathers, surplus
     Fat, his comb, wing weight, down to a mere
     Shadow, like a Graves bird ready to sing.
     For him every morning
     Paradise Merchant Mart reopened its doors
     With regular fire sales, Shoe Parlor
     Blackened its aroma, Professional
     Building ran its elevators up and down
     So fast that pulled teeth turned up in other mouths.

     Activity. The tax base broadened in the sunlight
     As gradually sun spreads wider after coffee.
     It was a busy world on that side of the road,
     For which the entrepreneur chicken was in his able
     Way responsible.
     At noon, loans, mortgages, personal interest,
     At night notarized after-images, as if by sundown
     The elevator had turned to moving sidewise
     Frames and phrases to be read and reread.

     He was not boss or mayor, but he certainly was
     Right on that spinning wheel which spun the public
     In and out of his stores, and his pleasantries
     Began to spin the flesh right off his bones.
     That is why the chicken began to sing
     High, not loud, and why transparencies
     Of pipestems were his legs, his beak aloft,
     His feathers lean, drawing the busy air,
     And why he crossed the road.

In dialogues of modus vivendi:

I. Four old men standing around in the yard,
    Part in the shade, part sun, pretty old,
    And talking about if in their lives
    They had ever been sick.
    One said he had been sick many times,
    About every two years in fact, one thing or another.
    One said he had one big sickness—
    A busted leg kept him off engines a year.

    One said he was mighty healthy, but back in '18
    At the time of the flu epidemic, he had the flu.
    The boss came up to him at work and said,
    You look pretty seedy. I don't want any flu around here.
    I'll take you home in my car. Well sir,
    That was the first time he'd ridden in a car,
    But he was proud, and when he saw a streetcar coming,
    One of those old yellow cars, he said, boss let me off here.
    At the other end of the line he had to walk fifteen blocks,
    And when he got home, he fell on his face,
    And his wife screamed at him, like Yi! Yi!
    Because he was never sick.

    The fourth said, I remember
    One of the many times I was sick
    And the doctor came. He had his office
    In his house, a white house like that there on the hill.
    Now they are all in tall risers,
    Or these ranch buildings set up with flowers.
    He told me, it's the annual state of your blood.
    I think about that, annual, semiannual,
    It gives me confidence. They agreed:
    Annual, semiannual, that's the whole of it.

II. Blast, says the neighbor at the gate,
      Yesterday I called up Dr. Trax
      In Engineering, transferred me over
      To Dr. Trox in Metallurgy, what I wanted
      Was a press to press a million pounds of weight
      On this niobium, to gauge its flow. *Never heard of it.*
      Well it was discovered in 1907, I said.
      But not workable. Well that remains to be seen,
      If you've got the press. Also I need steel for a mold
      Strong enough to withstand that pressure. Would 282 do?
      Never heard of it. Is this the Metallurgy Department?
      What would you do with niobium if you did work it?
      Well—thanks anway. Hasn't ever heard of space metals.

      You speak of a resistant piece of metal;
      Mind's more; when new facts
      Ask a man to shift his thought, he stiffens.
      Every groove of assumption
      Digs deeper down to the heart of his head.

      Well, even without the press I can learn something.
      For instance, when I hammer a piece of this stuff
      After it's been melted in the electric beam
      And shaped into ingots, I note it flows
      From the center to the margins. This means it can be compressed.
      Yet the underside I can't even dent. Why?
      A sloppy melting job is the answer.
      Where will the first fractures come?
      Right at the margins, where the hammered metal
      Flows out to the rigid base. I predict this,
      But more I'd like to prevent it
      Before it takes the shape of an instrument in a plane
      On a joblot order.

So I would
Like to prevent the gobblegook we get
Out of our flawed sense, our inertia, of concept,
Whether we speak or mouth our language. It's beautiful
As your candy bar of metal, your foil,
It gleams, it moves, it conducts, it shapes itself,
It speaks to the moon quick as niobium.
But we do not understand it, let it lie
Flat and fractured in our firm heads.
It isn't the work I mind, it's the obstructionists.
What are they there for, to hold back the future
Till it struggles out with a PhD in the past?
The leaves keep coming back out on the trees, you notice,
Though they're not in the departmental files.

I grew up in Ulster, watching the blacksmiths
Flail their shoes into the evening dark
Till I fell asleep, but I learned a lot as I fell.
One thing an old Ulsterman won't take is red tape,
He likes hot iron. Hear Mrs. Moore's piano speaking up?
We better get back to work.

III. The studies you tend to favor—
     Of the church in the Reformation,
     Of endocrine regulation
     In the shaping up of the skull?
     Of the growth of recrystallized grains
     In several high-purity metals,
     The writing of Eliot's novels,
     And the pathogens of maize?
     Decay modes of neutral K-mesons,
     Applied dispersion relations,
     Orlando Furioso,

And the Red Jungle Fowl?
        Creative fictions!

No, rather Australian reptiles,
Igneous rocks near Oslo,
Modern anti-utopian literature
And studies of the changing scene,
Methods for improving decisions
In the Atlantic Community.
Respiratory physiology,
Italian humanist creed.
Early American theater,
Suicide in the Japanese forces,
G.E. Moore, English philosopher,
And the propagation of waves.
        Theories of imagination!

Let us bargain: micrometeorology,
Time as a structural principle,
The British Labour Party,
Records of ocean tides.
Phonology of spoken Latin,
Theory of spin resonance,
Representations of finite
Groups in rings of integers,
Two-dimensional theories
Of thin elastic shells.
The Austrian military border
In Croatia and Slovenia,
The five-carbonate fraction
Of deep-sea sedimentations,
The Song of Songs, which is Solomon's,
The concept of design!

IV.   CASTOR: Planetary! That is my vision.
            I see the nebulae wheeling
            Over the crash and clatter of this office building
            Tumultuous the view. See—
            Look between those two trees there—up—up
            That spiral dust—
            That is the ur-matter radiant, of which we are
                made.

    ROMULUS: Say it in sextuplicate   REMUS:
            If you're going to say it
            Don't fool around with duplicate   —tuplicate
            Say it in sextuplicate
            Play it or sophisticate   —tuplicate
            But play it play it play it
            Say it in sextuplicate   —tuplicate
            If you're going to say it.

    REBECCA: I couldn't care less about your records.
            I feel you suggest an outmoded era—
            The jazz machine—all that repetition—
            The file and turntable. Fortunately
            Into machinery has come the concept now
            Of the unique. This is what I am.
            Note that while some of you direct your sights
                toward the heavens,
            And others cant and recant what is before you
            In endless chains of records,
            I sit by myself, turned inward,
            Just being. Feedback here becomes organic
            An entity in itself. I. Unique.
            I speak in English only as persona,
            As all the world's a stage. Actually
            My own language is the one I speak
            With most love, but it's at decibels
            Beyond the range of all but dolphins.

Dolphins! Do you know them? Charming!

DR. ANTHONY: Gentlemen, Ladies, will you join me at the
conference table?

I'm having Miss Coffee-Maker make us a little
coffee.

We have a difficult matter to discuss this morning,
To speak figuratively: Denmark.
What is rotten in the state of Denmark?
Not murder. At least not in the sense of regicide,
But I could term it murder by delay.
We're just not cutting the mustard, that's the
upshot.
We're not putting the baby buggies out on the
line;
Why? That is my question to you this morning.
Why?

TONTO: ———

POLLUX: Planetary, that is my vision.
See the ur-dust spiraling up there?
That is the radiant Denmark
Of which we are made.

V. You must go no further in this dangerous way
You must play less, talk less, hold fast
Get your affairs in order, straighten your heart.
Do you hear me?
Yes, I hear you.

How about a business school, something like that?
Computer machine operators get excellent pay.
A little discipline from morning to night
Is what you need. Do you hear me?
Yes, I hear you.

Seriously, kid, I wish you'd get up off that chair
Get your nose out of that book, you won't find anything there.
So real is the real reality about you everywhere
Do you hear?
     Yes, I hear.

Yes, I hear you, father, but what you are trying to say
You must not say. I wrap up in ennui
Every moment I listen, to hold away
These lies you lie to me. Do you hear me?
     Son, do you hear me?

Yes, I hear you, father. But I must forbid
These impositions from above, these ex cathedra
Pronunciamentos. It is time you tried
To sense a beat of life not before known,
To your cagey rib. Do you hear me?

I am one of your new fathers—You are right.
Another—It is time for a new suit.
Another—For a new look, for a new book.
Another—For a new leaf, for a new view.
Another—For a new you, a new me and you.

Fathers, I hear you. Where is my old one,
My old pa gone?
Fathers, I hear your terrible shiny speed
And your new greed.
You must go no further in this dangerous way,
Talk less, hold fast. Do you hear me?
     Dear old pa, do you hear me?

40

We have the generation which carries something new not far enough,
　　And then the generation which carries it too far,
　　And then the generation which brings it back again.

　　Do I think of something and do you not understand it?
　　And does it brew along without momentum, and does finally
　　It take its place and move like sorghum in a slow slide

　　To the future, or do you yelp
　　Those absolutes of last degrees
　　Without which we are impatient? Come on! Come on!

　　Or do we recall a past complete, golden and still,
　　Toward which we tired turn and bring again
　　Our brilliant splendors to its ample sill?

　　We have the body which retells
　　Ontogeny through all its narrow cells,
　　Phylogeny through all its harrowed wills.

The life of Galileo as it is reset
    On a lecture platform allows us lecturers
    To step back one pace and find ourselves
    Under rope or miter.

    Investiture occurs not to the tolling
    Of a recanting bell, merely
    To our campanile striking
    Its familiar schedule.

    Ugly truth, lovely value take us
    Into their cast, while around their
    Moving inquisitions
    Move the inquisitive spheres.

What do you think caused the disaster here
        In 1906? Earthquake or fire?
        Tremor or blaze? At least they were natural.
        We did not teach them. When we were fighting them
        Then we were fighting the waves.

        Formerly we made Satan jump up from hell mouth,
        Rushing in black and red. We belabored him,
        We beat him back. Even Faust finally
        Ascended, shaking dust from his feet.
        Then, not much later, we were fighting the waves.

        Now our attacker in gray and silver
        Is a machine. He runs scarlet ribbons
        Into a tape, he manufactures
        Mouth stretchers ready for screams.
        Binary, he believes we are one or nothing
        Though we are fighting.

        We may say it was he whose faulty altimeter
        Dropped Dag Hammarskjöld down over Africa.
        Demon or disaster, all the same to us
        Who we are blaming.
        But Hammarskjöld would not. When his sons came to him
        He would not fight them, he went to draw them
        Free from the waves.

I fear to take a step; along the edge
  Of this precipice on which we balance, bearing our burdens,
  Fingers appear, clutching; they are the climbers
  From below, as we were, to this ample ledge.

  May be when we go higher, on to some plateau
  Filled with flowers, we will stoop and reach
  Down to their hands as once one stooped to ours.
  But now I fear to step, to see the faces
  Of those who take the fingers under their heels.

After noon I lie down
        As if my spine were bent from burdens,
        My mind from abundance,
        Straitening into easy quiet.

        After fifty years this is the profit,
        That the weight of goods
        Dozes me off. But what wakes me
        Is the fright that ones thirty, twenty, are sleeping also.

        They are yawning against the clatter of the day,
        Its rash signs as they read them, and draw
        Into a restful silence,
        A sleep in the sun.

        On the world's other side, the shadow
        Darkest before dawn is darkening
        Before dawn, and sleepers in their night
        Waken with desperation for daylight.

        We have it. It crackles down our freeways
        As if to consume us. Is in our daylight
        Someone awake enough to take, use,
        Share its garish inequities?

Marin mousebait contains warfarin.
　　What does its ratbait contain? Yes,
　　That's why we have to dig holes against rat blast.

　　When my son Tommy flew off the garage
　　As supermouse, he landed on his feet.
　　In a bed of double petunias.

　　That was lucky.
　　Warfarin is enough,
　　Without the superstuff.

Daniel Boone stepped up to a window
    (What! a window?) with his trusty rifle,
    And he shot his bear.
    This was some bear.
    It was a millionaire,
    A Harvard, London, and a South Sea bear
    A French, a football bear.

    A corporate family
    And incorporate party,
    Thoroughly transistized
    Into his rocking chair,
    Built and bureaucratized,
    Daddied and deared and dared,
    Indomitable bear.

    What an investment
    Of time, of love too,
    All in one body,
    A computation
    Of maximal purpose,
    A one-man world.

    Daniel is angry
    That after the eighth grade
    This bear should travel
    So far ahead.
    Unfair
    That a bear
    Should rock so big a chair.

So gets him, and as he is got
Shows him
Shows us
It takes no complicated bomb or plot
To win again us back to wilderness,
But just one pot, pure, individual, shot.

As difference blends into identity
    Or blurs into obliteration, we give
    To zero our position at the center,
    Withdraw our belief and baggage.

    As rhyme at the walls lapses, at frontiers
    Customs scatter like a flight of snow,
    And boundaries moonlike draw us out, our opponents
    Join us, we are their refuge.

    As barriers between us melt, I may treat you
    Unkindly as myself, I may forget
    Your name as my own. Then enters
    Our anonymous assailant.

    As assonance by impulse burgeons
    And that quaver shakes us by which we are spent,
    We may move to consume another with us,
    Stir into parity another's cyphers.

    Then when our sniper steps to a window
    In the brain, starts shooting, and we fall surprised,
    Of what we know not do we seek forgiveness
    From ourselves, for ourselves?

In the town where every man is king,
　　Every man has one subject,
　　Every man bends to his own foot.
　　Bring on the mirror that he may properly bend.
　　But who will bring it on?

　　In the castle where is no hunger and no need,
　　Every man gives gifts and receives
　　Gifts. But of these only his own
　　Enhance him, the ring giver.
　　He must wear his ring.

　　Gradually, as he resolves the oppression of his edicts,
　　Losing his fellow lords to dim perspectives,
　　Monoliths of rock and stone, even
　　Of reinforced concrete, become before him
　　Mirrors. He licks the glass.

I walked along the river path, the river
  I never lived beside,
  And met there, hook and line, king of that kingdom
  I would not recognize.

  He was the golden branch of Eliot, of
  Those wasteland parties where I had to play
  Tiresias, and he was a king
  Whom I did not believe.

  Laius nor any man's killed by his son
  Unless he wills it, so I said
  To this old bird where he sat, Why let come riding
  The handsomest of your brood to do you in?

  And he wept, Because it is him or me—
  Should he not survive me, he survives not
  All that I was: alcoholic
  At forty, cheat at forty-five,
  Coward at fifty, these he will be

  Over again in sequence, while I sit
  Mourning myself in him. Tell him to hurry.
  That was the waste land as it dawned upon me
  To see it was my friend sat by the river
  Crouching and fishing in his father's form.

Throwing his life away,
    He picks at and smells it.
    Done up. When did I do this up?
    I date its death to the time someone
    Said something.
    Back then.
    Everything else, all striving, making,
    Marrying, error,
    Is this old bird.
Pah! He throws it.
    As the long string lengthens
    Out of his hand,
    It begins unwinding
    The ligaments of his hand.

So you are thinking of principles to go on,
　　　Principles of controversy, Alexander Meiklejohn says,
　　　Sitting in lamplight briskly, as late November
　　　Collects about him. Well, I will give you one.
　　　One is enough. Coherence.

　　　Coherence of agreement and difference,
　　　Wave and particle, concept and image,
　　　Exuberant complement I give you, not contrary,
　　　To keep a precarious gritty life between chaos
　　　And bland entropy, in which we can prevail.

　　　Our mien of survival, to know our separate natures
　　　And allow them. Allow
　　　Dividing light. Let be
　　　Candle and galaxy; the first word of them, logos,
　　　The wish to be.

　　　　　Alec, agreed. The soft rain quickens
　　　　In the increasing twilight. But what about fights?
　　　　What about sorties, annihilations,
　　　　Eyeball to eyeball confrontations,
　　　　And competition in the life of trade?

　　　　　Why, a game needs rivals and a rival makes
　　　　The world green. But grant a plain clash
　　　　In a single world, true contradiction, then it rests
　　　　Upon degree, remoteness
　　　　Of one sight from another within that world.

　　　　I say I see a bluejay on the roof
　　　　Across the way. You do not. Do I contradict you?
　　　　Then I come to stand where you stand,

Use your eyes, see what you see, a blue pipe.
But yes from where I was, it looked like a bird.

Bird, a good name for a small blue object
On a roof. Does it flutter, stir?
Even if it did, you might say
That's not a bird, not much of a bird I mean,
In my country are real birds, bluer than that.

To live a life out is to learn the ways
Of action in which we undertake the reach
Of knowing. The different lines of fact
To follow out, to cling to, when the sense
Of footing falls away.

To know where we are free and where determined,
So not to imprint one feather on another,
To know how the bees of atoms hum in the table,
A universe of spaces,
Yet steady our glasses on their giant wings.

To know the world within, and there confound
Self-contradiction in its knot of splendor,
And let its science say,
You are a committee, meet and negotiate,
Teauton.

Alec, myself I meet, but in what meeting?
Of many meetings? Of error, say? Well, push
The wrong-way car back over the line before impact.
Of planned aggression? Then try to intensify
The hoped-for suffering, to its desirers.

Of rare real contradiction? Then discover
The differences of degree that separate
One view from the other, and so celebrate
The fortunate variance, the happy fall,
And light to contemplate the difference by.

The trouble stirs at the limits of a life.
Mind starts in the dark to see what it can see,
Its hope marked plainly in nucleic code.
The bear goes over the mountain, and next day
Roams out of Eden entirely.

I seek fullness, I seek the complement
Of all I know, and it will not be still.
It will beget Abel and Cain if you will,
Who will say, Complement is a rarity;
We are engaged upon diversity.

Mediation has taken its move forward.
It notes not the surface arrogance
But the underlying regard.
The long destiny moving toward birth.
It can tell free speech from bound action.

It meets and holds the long birch love of goodness,
The long birch taste of guilt.
It takes the fierce birch blush of conscience
Into the open world in price of power,
Asking its name and even enemy.

Discourse makes signs to us, all signs of trouble,
To come between us and obliteration.
Trouble preserves the world and tells its name

Stemming from early day,
From early night.

Alec, the night comes in
Upon the lamp, and you determined and free
Open the door to it and bring it in. We're late,
The telephone rings, trouble on every hand
Seeks your agility, and makes you smile.

From Hindi:

I. A star quivered in a corner of the sky.
    I thought, yes
    everything sometime or other will shine out like this.

    A pebble stirred
    the water of the drowsy waves.
    I knew
    at least for once inertia will be shaken.

    Blossoms flowered
    in the deeps of forests,
    their fragrance spoke out, yes
    once at least I scatter and bestow.

    What more to ask
    than images of my aspiration—
    but belief needs none,
    a dream is better;
    what can an image do but shine or scatter,
    what will it offer?

                    —"A Star Quivered," by Kirti Chan-huri

II. ... But the accursed twilight came,
    brought with it the bad spirits of past memories
    and a shabby dusk.

    All of a sudden, as if wet fuel started smoking,
    as if that sort of smoke rose up from the houses
    in a spiral, with a dark hazy line behind it,
    mind and eyes burned with bitter tears.

This twilight, with somewhere a patch of light
but mostly darkness prevailing,
increased, as if building a fence of giant size
for a giant with no heart.
I felt that my life was in a cage
with ostriches, tigers, bears, wild dogs around me,
my life inextricably set in the accursed twilight.

—"You Are Alone," by Ajit Kumar

III. My father,
　　　a conquered Everest,

my mother,
　　　an ocean of milk poisoned with poverty,

my brother,
　　　a lion cub cinched up as a pack animal,

my sister,
　　　a doll made out of soiled clothes,

and I,
　　　a kettle of water
　　　boiling away to vapor,
　　　water consumed into vapor.

"The Family," by Vishwanath

58

Looking over toward Tamalpais,
    I could see cars crossing its Sunday shoulder
    Over to picnic. Metal by metal
    Scratched the light, moved clear over
    And I would join them.

    Then a wind rose, a dun cloud
    Came across, and I thought quickly
    How to treat a house in a tornado?
    Close down tight, crouch in a corner,
    Or open up the doors and let her ride?

    The cloud was in the house, a crowd of shouters,
    A kind of club on an outing over this way.
    Rushing, protesting, they kept saying
    Where's the rest of the house, where's the rest of it?
    Sundays of the kind they used to be.

Along the street where we used to stop for bread,
    There used to walk
    A leathery megalomanic dwarf, playing
    At directing traffic.

    Up we would drive and park, and I would promise
    Every time to say hello to him,
    But did not,
    Nor did his wild eyes ever look,

    But snap and spark,
    And the best I managed
    Was a pale smile in his direction,
    Which was nowhere.

    That leathern skin, pinched eye, dumb jaw,
    I saw, I see, in the somewhat deprived,
    And every time I am heartsick to claim it.

    And so am reasonable, yes indeed, but of course, to be sure.
    Oh, rebels against reason, where do you fly?
    To my wild dwarf on his drug? I will have him greet you.

Dear Frank, Here is a poem
    I dreamed of you last night;
    It makes me happy
    Because it makes sense to me.

    We went to the Greek Theater to see a play
    And as we entered were given elaborate menus
    Of the players' names.
    Dinner was three dollars.
    It was served on the little round tables from cocktail lounges.

    I kept leaning back against your knees,
    Because of those backless benches, and you kept moving
    Further and further away in the amphitheater,
    I following, until finally you said,
    Jo: I am having the six dollar dinner.

Still early morning, the wind's edge
    Catches in veins the edges that stick in them;
    Thorny friends, burrs of confusion,
    Pressures of office that take a rhomboid wrench
    Through every breath. I would, I say,
    To the genii that live in the long lamp of hope,
    Have them all rounded, is that not possible?

    All edges rounded till they will bubble
    Easily together? Slowly the sun,
    Rising up over the roofs and trees,
    Brings another way beyond my wish.
    The edges meet and fit, the angles turn
    To complement, merge and sparkle, vein to vein,
    As the sharp morning seeks delineation.

When Sanders brings feed to his chickens, some sparrows
    Sitting and rocking in the peach tree at the fence corner
    By the chicken house, fly up
    And shoot off to another tree farther away,
    An acacia. The whole air
    Is shaken by their mass motion.

    But then one leaf of the empty peach tree stirs
    And I see in it one sparrow sitting still.
    Is he a guard? absent-minded? averse
    To mass motion? Rather, he may enjoy
    The comings and goings
    Of Sanders to the chickens.

Apart from branches in courtyards and small stones,
    The countryside is beyond me.
    I can go along University Avenue from Rochester to Sobrante
    And then the Avenue continues to the Bay.

    Often I think of the dry scope of foothill country,
    Moraga Hill, Andreas, Indian country, where I was born
    And where in the scrub the air tells me
    How to be born again.

    Often I think of the long rollers
    Breaking against the beaches
    All the way down the coast to the border
    On bookish cressets and culverts blue and Mediterranean.

    There I break
    In drops of spray as fine as letters
    Blown high, never to be answered,
    But waking am the shore they break upon.

    Both the dry talkers, those old Indians,
    And the dry trollers, those old pirates,
    Say something, but it's mostly louder talking,
    Gavel rapping, and procedural dismays.

    Still where we are, and where we call and call,
    The long rollers of the sea come in
    As if they lived here. The dry Santa Ana
    Sweeps up the town and takes it for a feast.

    Then Rochester to El Sobrante is a distance
    No longer then my name.

When the sun came, the rooster expanded to meet it,
    Stood up, stirred his wings,
    Raised his red comb and sentence
    Rendered imperative utterance
    Saying, Awake. Nothing answered.
    He took in a beakful of air; yes, first it was he,
    And engendered a number of hard-shelled cacklers,
    One for each day in the week.
    They grew in their yard, the dust in their feathers,
    Who heard them praise him? An egg.

    In the night, in the barn, the eggs wakened and cried,
    Saying, We have been wakened,
    And cried, saying Father, so named him,
    His feathers and beak from the white and the yolk.
    Father, who newly can ring out the welkin,
    And crow, we will listen to hear.
    As toward him we move, and the wings of our feathers grow
        bright,
    And we spring from the dust into flame
    He will call us his chickens.
    But that was already their name.

How goes a crowd where it goes?
    Ten or a dozen, along a road?
    Each wavers.

    Some ramble on the road's shoulder,
    Some lean in, brush or confer, confidential,
    Some hold the center as it marks the way.

    Which is the group's line to its exact
    Destination? The ramblers
    Have to disclose it.

The leaf is growing,
      But not before your eyes like a motor scooter,
      Because it is still,
      More like a hand than a stone.

      What about stone?
      It is growing
      Before your eyes like a motor scooter,
      Not like a leaf but a hand.

      A hand? In it are growing
      A leaf and a stone, and grow still
      From the hand when it's gone
      Buzzing off like a motor scooter.

Does the world look like a park to you? Yes, almost suddenly
　　The world looks like a park.
　　Are there worn spots in the shorn grass? Yes, under
　　The childrens' feet,
　　And under the feet of bison behind trees.

　　Are there temperature controls in the park? Yes, the warm sun
　　Is made shady, and the warm shade
　　Sunny. Feelings too,
　　Whether out on the shorn lawns or behind the bushes,
　　Run hot and cold to the edges of Africa and Chicago.

　　It is a national park, then? Yes, national
　　In its red, white, and blue bunting, in its scope and convenience.
　　Hear the bears groping for sliced bacon.
　　In the national parks, however, the turbulence
　　Still perseveres, of waters?

　　Glaciers and gorges move down to the warm lawns?
　　Yes, but just to the point where the dams take them. Then they
　　　　ripple
　　Over the flooded farms of the Havasupai,
　　Of Nefertiti and Osiris,
　　And carry them softly off to the park's museums.

Every day when she came to the steps that led
    To the class to be taught,
    The bells in the tower were telling the cost of the hour,
    And there they met.
    They were ready and she was ready.

    One day, by a lost minute or so, she came
    To the silent spot
    Where she waited the bells to ring and they did not,
    The future fallen bells, but had flown
    Into a past over and done.

    Where had the unsounded hour gone?
    It was ready and she was ready.

I am trying to think what it means to be right.
I am trying to think what good means,
Goods mean.
I have come from the uncertainties of childhood, school, and
foreign travel
To my familiar husband, daughters, and sons,
In my familiar low-lying home alight with flowers
And my beige car and hair.
Why am I good?
Because I have worked with intensest devotion,
With patience unstinting, seldom with anger,
And with a tremendous strain at understanding
Toward this purpose: toward these good sons,
Shining daughters, husband content.
How does the world corrupt them past my hand?

I wake at the third alarm that the dawn will never
Come again, that in some terror
The bedstead will overthrow the light.
In forced lamplight I wander among the sofas
And read headlines of the death of God.
God, you have stood
By my side, you have held my hand
From cruelties,
You have guided my steps
In the gentlest ways,
You have said to my heart, rest.
Work and rest. Love and rest.

Now you move off, where?
Leaving at my side, in my garden furniture,
Many lives other than mine, who do not know me
And I do not know them.
You bring me into the heart of my living room

And you open a window on a world
In which it was not built.
The flames that burn me
From some hurled cocktail
From some sick son, other son?
From some soft southern voice, soft asian robe,
Burn them, by a choice I cannot conceive.

Are you evil as well? You leave
Heaven in spite
And then rise back to it with coal on coal
Casting the heavy flames on carpet floors?
If my old father, my happy husband were you,
If I were you,
Could we not keep goodness for our good,
Could we not
Let others, when they will, trade with hell,
The neighbors' boy, the citizens of the left,
All trouble seekers, let them seek
And find, but not in heaven?

Heavenly color
In television strikes the colors of blood,
The screen burns among trees during dinner.
The dog that worries for Associated Gas
Assumes the presidency.
Now I must lay me
Again to sleep, the soul you take to keep
Youthful still, trembles.
The yard outside, world outside cry.
If it is right and good
Where you are,
Why are you not here?

Bucking and rolling, the ship bent
    Over the curve of the world,
    Round, round, the gulls flapped,
    Sails flapped,
    Round, they called out to Columbus, as cinnamon
    Filled the imaginative Atlantic air.

    The speechless microscope of Hooke opened
    Cells of cork, not calling but being round,
    The dense
    Peripheral regions of its cytoplasm
    Round the watery vacuoles,
    The sweet breath of oxygen over sugar.

    Round, says a life, rustle of dividing life,
    Upon the curve
    Of morning's coming back,
    A morning first to see one thought turning
    In expectation
    Its aromatic line.

In the neighborhood of my childhood, a hundred lungers
    Coughed in their tents like coyotes.
    The sand was dry and saged with mesquite.
    Even so, from mountains the dew dropped
    Down on the canvas in the early dark.
    The kerosene puffed away as I fell to sleep.

    In that rich landscape I was deprived,
    Because no negro coughed among the tents, moved
    Outward among the distant orange groves.
    A square shot of Indians walked the coals,
    But so pure the absence of black skin, I thought
    All the sorrows of the world were white.

    Later, a stonewall neighbor Harriman's
    Krazy Kat neither spoke to us, nor spoke
    To any negro neighbor because we had none.
    Mexican squatters in the boxes in the dry river
    Sent no drift of blackness to our dream.
    Black Sambo was our child.

    When land gave no relief, across the plains
    The white and blistered figures in jalopies
    Moved into town, but did not come to college.
    And so who were they? Such an array
    In sandy paleness needed to be brown.
    Minority, myself.

    Deprived.
    Out of the sunny and the shadowy scenes
    Where I look back with wonderment and love,
    An oversimple marginal deployment
    Of absence,
    A relentless letting be.

Down from another planet they have settled to mend
    The Hampton Institute banisters. They wear bow ties and braces.
    The flutings they polish with a polished hand.

    Wingless, they build and repair
    The mansions of what we have thought to be our inheritance.
    Caution and candor they labor to maintain.

    They are out of phase. I prepare
    To burn all gentle structures, greek or thatch,
    Under the masterful torch of my president here and abroad,

    Till stubble outsmolders, and muslim and buddhist crack
    In the orbit of kiln.
                    A smoke
    To some calm Christian planet will drift,

    To where they are mending their mansions, beside of whose doors
    They are standing at ease, they are lifting the fans
    Of unburdenable wings.

Yesterday evening as the sun set late,
>We parked at Land's End, past the Golden Gate,
>To see the cypress lean in from that ocean,
>And the wave-path lengthen to the lengthening sun.
>In the VW over beside us, a yellow-haired girl
>Looked at us with a radiance
>Hardly receivable. We smiled and turned
>Back to the sea as she held out her arms to us.
>Her blown voice said to the three with her,
>I know why you brought me here,
>To love these mixed-up people, and I do!
>See, they are smiling at me, poor sad
>Mixed-up people! Her friends sheltering
>Walked with her to the cliff's edge.
>Deep to the rocks, far to the falling sun,
>She reached her hand. She saw her hand,
>Held it close to her eyes, widened its fingers,
>Hand translucent. Who will keep it? She put it
>Inside the coat of the yellow-haired boy and he leaned
>Over her like the wind.
>When she came back to the car she had lost her hand,
>Lost us. We said goodbye as they drove off.
>A trawler crossed between us and the sun.

When I was eight, I put in the left-hand drawer
    Of my new bureau a prune pit.
    My plan was that darkness and silence
    Would grow it into a young tree full of blossoms.

    Quietly and unexpectedly I opened the drawer a crack
    And looked for the sprouts; always the pit
    Anticipated my glance, and withheld
    The signs I looked for.

    After a long time, a week, I felt sorry
    For the lone pit, self-withheld,
    So saved more, and lined them up like an orchard.
    A small potential orchard of free flowers.

    Here memory and storage lingered
    Under my fingerprints past retrieval,
    Musty and impatient as a prairie
    Without its bee.

    Some friends think of this recollection
    As autobiography. Others think it
    A plausible parable of computer analysis.
    O small and flowering orchard of free friends!

Truth is never
      always
      at times
          ugly.
O absolute,
We find in you the harmony you demand.
O counter,
Snarl at necessity.
O friend.

Have I outgrown you?
    Have we lived in a little city together
    And now while you map your local entertainments
    Do I go out upon some new portage,
    Desperate to be lonelier and beyond,
    Wealthier to ascend?

    You write that things are going well in town and I see them
    Going well. But by what luminant?
    Bobby, see Jane jump; Eve, Adam. Clearly
    Temptation brings the light so full to bear
    That you and semblance have the same substance.
    Am I going away to your nearest distance?

THE WESLEYAN POETRY PROGRAM

Distinguished contemporary poetry in cloth and paperback editions

ALAN ANSEN: *Disorderly Houses* (1961)

JOHN ASHBERY: *The Tennis Court Oath* (1962)

ROBERT BAGG: *Madonna of the Cello* (1961)

ROBERT BLY: *Silence in the Snowy Fields* (1962)

TURNER CASSITY: *Watchboy, What of the Night?* (1966)

TRAM COMBS: *saint thomas. poems.* (1965)

DONALD DAVIE: *Events and Wisdoms* (1965); *New and Selected Poems* (1961)

JAMES DICKEY: *Buckdancer's Choice* (1965) [National Book Award in Poetry, 1966]; *Drowning With Others* (1962); *Helmets* (1964)

DAVID FERRY: *On the Way to the Island* (1960)

ROBERT FRANCIS: *The Orb Weaver* (1960)

JOHN HAINES: *Winter News* (1966)

RICHARD HOWARD: *The Damages* (1967); *Quantities* (1962)

BARBARA HOWES: *Light and Dark* (1959)

DAVID IGNATOW: *Figures of the Human* (1964); *Say Pardon* (1961)

DONALD JUSTICE: *Night Light* (1967); *The Summer Anniversaries* (1960) [A Lamont Poetry Selection]

CHESTER KALLMAN: *Absent and Present* (1963)

LOU LIPSITZ: *Cold Water* (1967)

JOSEPHINE MILES: *Kinds of Affection* (1967)

VASSAR MILLER: *My Bones Being Wiser* (1963); *Wage War on Silence* (1960)

W. R. MOSES: *Identities* (1965)

DONALD PETERSEN: *The Spectral Boy* (1964)

HYAM PLUTZIK: *Apples from Shinar* (1959)

VERN RUTSALA: *The Window* (1964)

HARVEY SHAPIRO: *Battle Report* (1966)

JON SILKIN: *Poems New and Selected* (1966)

LOUIS SIMPSON: *At the End of the Open Road* (1963) [Pulitzer Prize in Poetry, 1964]; *A Dream of Governors* (1959)

JAMES WRIGHT: *The Branch Will Not Break* (1963); *Saint Judas* (1959)